I'm Reading About

KENTUCKY

The Bluegrass State!

GALLOPADE

by Carole Marsh

Printed and Manufactured in Peachtree City, GA., USA
www.gallopade.com

Book design: John Hanson

Editorial manager: Janice Baker

Kentucky is a great state.

It is one of a kind.

What makes Kentucky special?

Let's read about it and see!

Who lived in Kentucky first?

Native Americans did!

They moved around to find food.
They hunted in Kentucky's woods.
They fished in Kentucky's rivers.
They gathered fruits and seeds and nuts.

EXPLORERS

Explorers came to Kentucky in 1750.
They came from the colony of Virginia.

Dr. Thomas Walker was their leader.
He discovered a gap in the mountains.
He named it the "Cumberland Gap."

SETTLEMENT

A man named James Harrod came
to Kentucky in 1774.
He came from the colony of Pennsylvania.
He started the first settlement in Kentucky.
Its name was Harrodstown.

Harrodstown is known as
Harrodsburg today.

Harrodstown

STATEHOOD

Kentucky was the 15th state
to join the United States of America!

Isn't it great,
to be a state!
I bet Kentucky
could hardly wait!

Kentucky became a state in 1792.

Kentucky
The 15th
State
Here we are!

FLAG

I am the state flag.
I was adopted in 1962.

What color am I?
I am blue.

Look at me.
What else do you see?

I fly high over the state of Kentucky!

COMMONWEALTH OF KENTUCKY
UNITED WE STAND
DIVIDED WE FALL

CAPITAL

Say hello to Frankfort,
the capital city of Kentucky!

There is an important building in Frankfort.
It is the State Capitol.
Kentucky's laws are made there!

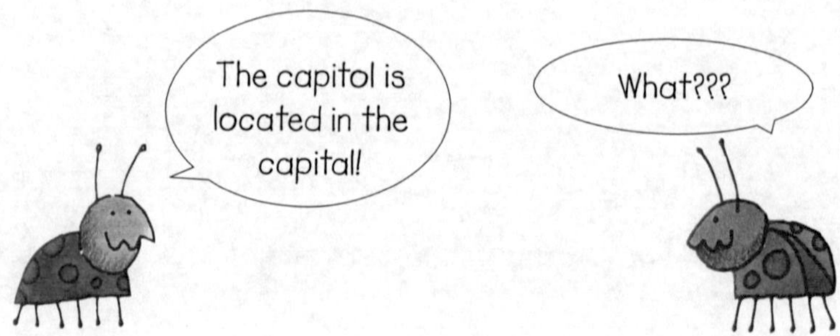

Capitol

SEAL

I am a seal,
but I am not the State Seal.
If I were, I would be very important.
I would be stamped on many official papers.
(Ouch, that might hurt!)

COMMONWEALTH OF KENTUCKY
UNITED WE STAND
DIVIDED WE FALL

Now, that's official!

NICKNAME

State nicknames are fun!
State nicknames are great!
They share fun facts
about each state!

Kentucky's nickname is "The Bluegrass State."

Horses like to eat Kentucky bluegrass!

The Bluegrass State

BORDERS

Look at Kentucky.
Kentucky is in a region called "the South."

Kentucky borders seven other states.
Find them on the map!

Borders

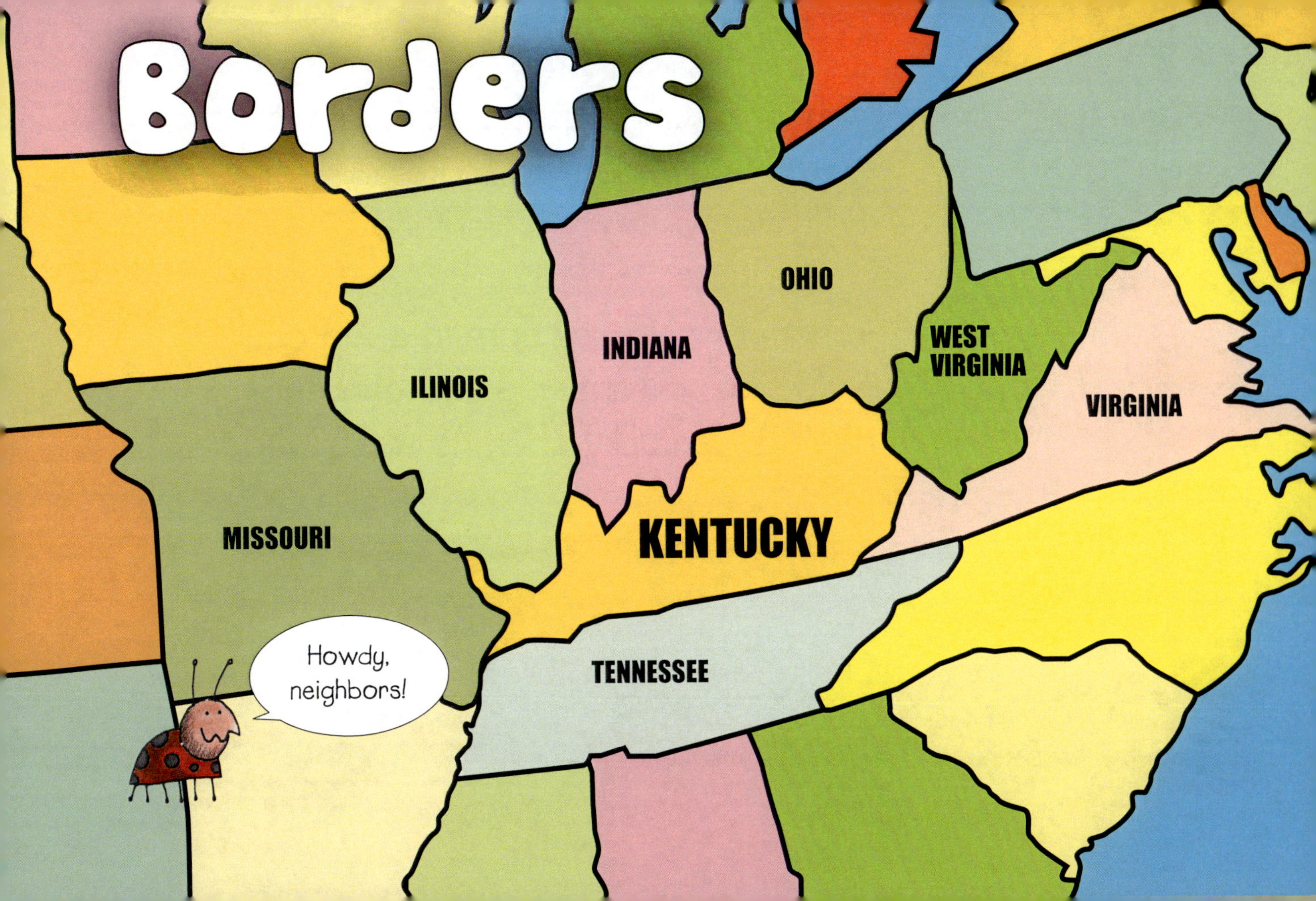
OHIO
INDIANA
WEST VIRGINIA
ILINOIS
VIRGINIA
MISSOURI
KENTUCKY
TENNESSEE
Howdy, neighbors!

PRESIDENT

Abraham Lincoln was the 16th President
of the United States.
He was born in Kentucky!

Abraham Lincoln was born in a log cabin.
His dad was a farmer and a carpenter.
His family left Kentucky when he was 7 years old.

Abraham Lincoln

PEOPLE

Many famous people

Daniel Boone

Pioneer who blazed new trails for settlers to come to Kentucky

Henry Clay

U.S. Senator who helped keep the Union together before the Civil War

Mary Todd Lincoln

First Lady and wife of Abraham Lincoln

call our state home!

Colonel Harland Sanders

Founder of Kentucky Fried Chicken

Martha Layne Collins

First woman governor of Kentucky

Muhammad Ali

Professional boxer known as one of the top athletes of the 20th century

PEOPLE

Cardinal

BIRD

I am the state bird, and I fly
over Kentucky, proud and high.

As I fly, up in the sky,
I flap my wings to tell you "Hi!"

The Kentucky state bird is the Cardinal.

Goldenrod

FLOWER

I am the Goldenrod.
I am the state flower.

I grow where it's warm and sunny.
I bloom in late summer.
I help make Kentucky beautiful!

Look at me! Smell me!
When I bloom, I turn fields into
blankets of yellow!

Tulip Poplar

TREE

I am a Tulip Poplar—I'm the state tree.
All over Kentucky is where you'll find me.

My roots run deep, they keep me strong.
I can live for hundred of years—that's very long!

I stand up straight, big and tall.
Don't climb too high—it would hurt to fall!

Honeybee

INSECT

I am the Honeybee.
I am the state agricultural insect.

I might sting you if you bother me,
But really, I am your friend.

I carry pollen from flower to flower.
I make honey.
I help Kentucky crops grow.

BZZZZZZZZZZZ!

Rivers

RIVERS

Kentucky has many rivers.
The Ohio River forms the northern border of the state.

The river habitat is home to many animals:

Birds **Deer** **Snakes** **Frogs** **Fish** **and More!**

Rivers were Kentucky's first highways.
People floated down the rivers on flatboats.
They carried goods to sell or trade!

Black Mountain

MOUNTAINS

Kentucky's mountains are the place to be.
Hiking, fishing, camping—
fun for you and me.

Winter weather brings lots of snow.
Temperatures drop to freezing and below!

Coal Mining

COALFIELDS

Kentucky has a valuable resource known as coal.
It is found deep under the ground.

Coal is very important to the world.
It is used to provide power for homes and businesses!

Coal is the official state mineral of Kentucky!

Mammoth Cave

LANDMARK

Kentucky has many caves.
Mammoth Cave is the most famous one.
It is the longest cave system in the world!

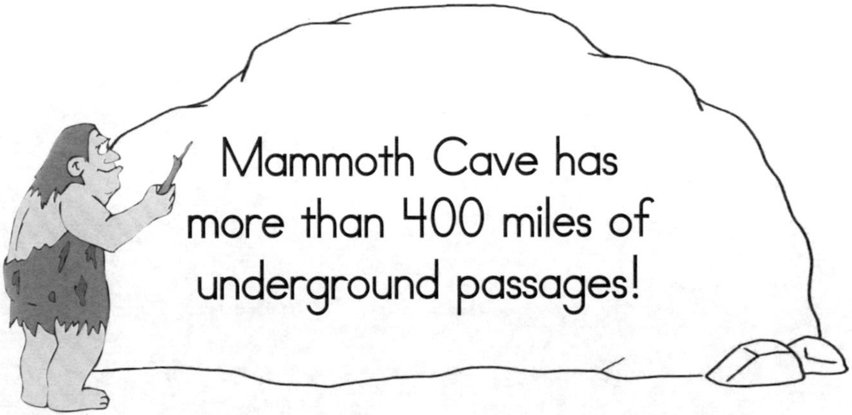

Kentucky Crops

Kentucky has many farms.
Why?
Because Kentucky has good soil and a warm climate!

Some of the top crops grown in Kentucky are:

Tobacco **Corn** **Soybeans** **Apples**

Sports in Kentucky

SPORTS

Baseball! Basketball! Football!
Kentucky has it all.

Whether you like to watch or play,
You are sure to have a ball!

Wildcats **Cardinals** **Colonels**

Eagles

Racers

Hilltoppers

& More!

Kentucky: Home of the Kentucky Derby

CLAIM TO FAME

The Kentucky Derby is the world's most famous horse race!
The race is run every year in May.
Horses race for $1\frac{1}{4}$ miles.
It only takes them about two minutes!

Most of the horses that have won the race were born in Kentucky!

GLOSSARY

climate: weather conditions in an area over a long period of time

colony: a settlement ruled by another country

elect: to choose someone by voting

habitat: a place where plants or animals naturally live

laws: rules made by the government

pollen: a yellow powder that helps plants make new plants

region: an area that has similar characteristics

resource: something found in nature that can be used by people

settlement: the first community in an area

thoroughbred: a breed of horse used in horse racing